The Giraffe

A Living Tower

by Christine and Michel Denis-Huot

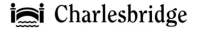 Charlesbridge

What animal can grow up to be 18 feet tall? The giraffe — it is the tallest living animal in the world!

African lookout

In the heat of the day, the giraffes stand in the shade of the trees. Suddenly, they stop chewing and shake their tails. They have spotted a person walking through the bush.

Immediately, the zebras and the gnus stop grazing and look around nervously. They know that this tail shaking is the signal for danger.

The long-necked giraffes are well equipped to see an enemy in the bushy savannahs of Africa. Giraffes do not like the dense forest where it is difficult to see and run away from danger. They also do not like open, bare plains where there are no trees to hide in or leaves to eat.

A giraffe can see a person over a mile away.

Acacia feast

Now that the hottest hours of the day are over, the giraffes walk off to find other trees to eat. Giraffes do not compete with other animals for food. With such a long neck, a giraffe can reach acacia leaves that are so high up that no other animal can reach them. Even if herds of gazelles, zebras, and wildebeests have grazed that area, the giraffe's supply of food is untouched.

Giraffes eat leaves, bark, flowers, and fruit.

One of the giraffe's favorite foods is the leaves of the acacia tree. The long thorns do not bother the giraffe at all.

6

Because its front legs are so long, the giraffe has a hard time eating grass. It prefers the leaves of bushes and trees.

Like a camel, a giraffe drinks a lot at one time and can go without drinking for several days.

At a river, the giraffes take turns drinking. To reach the water, a giraffe must spread apart its long front legs and lower its long neck. A lion could sneak up and pounce on a drinking giraffe. So, as quickly as possible, the giraffe will drink several gallons of water and get up.

Giraffes will even sleep standing up because it is safer.

This gazelle is called the giraffe-gazelle because of its long neck.

Even the stinging ants that build their nests on acacia trees do not prevent a giraffe from eating the leaves.

A giraffe's tongue is as rough as the roughest sandpaper.

A giant tongue

The giraffe eats during the day or the night. Its black tongue stretches out as much as 18 inches to get between the thorns. The tongue reaches the new leaf growth and gathers a bouquet that it brings back to its mouth.

When the new leaf growth is all gone, the giraffe moves on to the next acacia tree.

Giraffe families

There are two main types of markings on the fur of giraffes. *Reticulated* giraffes live in the northeastern part of Africa. They have large, even patterns of brown and white that look as if a brown animal were covered by a big, white net. *Blotched* giraffes live in central and southern parts of Africa. They are yellower and have irregular spots.

A group of giraffes may be all females. The males and females are together only during mating time. After mating, the male goes off on his own. It will be 15 months before the female gives birth. When the time comes, she goes off alone to the special hiding place she has chosen.

The male may be two or three feet taller than the female. Its horns are also much bigger.

10

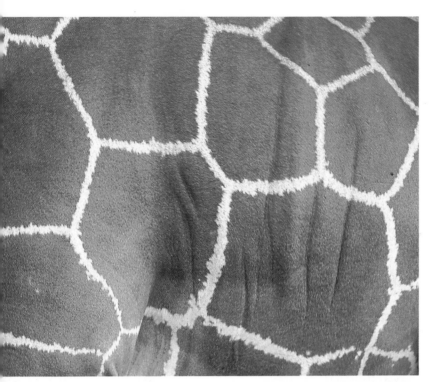

Reticulated giraffe

Just as we recognize each other by our faces, giraffes recognize each other by their spots.

Blotched giraffe

The baby weighs over 100 pounds at birth and is about 6 feet tall. The mother licks it to help it to stand up as quickly as possible.

Many baby giraffes are killed by hyenas and lions.

The young giraffe is a copy of the adult, except that in place of his future horns, he has tufts of black, bristly hairs.

A new life begins

The mother sniffs and licks her baby. The baby, moist and trembling, tries to raise his neck from the ground and to stand up . . . his long legs refuse to hold him.

Finally, he manages to stand and attempts a first step. The step leads to a stumble, and the baby finds himself nose down in the grass. When he is only one hour old, he can stand up long enough to find one of his mother's nipples and begin to drink. In just a few more hours, he will be ready to run.

A lioness is attracted by the smell of the baby giraffe. The mother faces the lion and kicks the ground violently with her front hooves. Knowing that one kick could kill it, the lioness retreats in defeat.

Baby face

The mother takes good care of her baby. She watches over him while he sleeps, and plays, and learns. He drinks milk from his mother several times a day.

By the time he is three weeks old, the baby has started to eat leaves.

When the mother wants to go find food for herself, she leaves the baby with another mother giraffe who babysits.

The little one grows quickly. He can grow as much as an inch taller in one day! In a year he will be more than nine feet tall!

"Hey, Mom, is this stuff good to eat?"

The baby stands to one side as he nurses. When he is frightened, he often runs to his mother or his "babysitter" and stands right under her.

14

'Hold still while I brush your mane, little one."

A giraffe can sleep with its eyes open or closed.

Danger! The mother and her baby gallop away together. They use their necks for balance as they gallop away at about 30 miles an hour!

A place to grow

The young giraffe, called a fawn, is very curious. He goes off to explore. He is interested in everything — bugs, birds, and lizards. He is not shy about meeting the animals who graze peacefully alongside the giraffes. These neighbors might be zebras, ostriches, impalas, elephants, or wildebeests. His mother cannot protect him from lions during these trips of exploration.

The fawn has two ways to escape from lions. He can run quickly to any adult giraffe who will defend him with powerful kicks. Or, he can stand so still that he blends in with his surroundings, making it impossible for a lion to see him. A giraffe's spots and colors look like bark and shadows through the leaves.

A bighearted giant

It's great to be two stories tall, but it can be a problem! When the giraffe leans down to drink, its head is six feet lower than its heart. If your head were suddenly lower than your heart, the blood would rush to your brain, and you would get dizzy. Fortunately, a giraffe has special valves which hold or release the blood according to the position of the giraffe's head.

Standing up is another problem for a giraffe. Its head is about 11 feet above its heart. That's a long way for its heart to have to pump the blood. That's why the giraffe has an enormous, strong heart weighing 25 pounds!

Better than a bath! The tickbird removes the pesky ticks and cleans the sores they leave.

Giraffes do not mind the heat. They do not perspire, which means that they do not get thirsty as fast as we do on a hot day.

18

The giraffe's long neck is not long enough to reach the water. Fortunately, it gets most of the water it needs from its food so it doesn't need to drink often.

When two males join a group of females, the males compete to see which one is the strongest.

The two males challenge one another, heads held high, ready for combat.

The males push each other with their necks and their heads.

The males do not use their hooves when they fight with each other. Usually, neither one is injured.

Competition between males

The life of the males is not always peaceful. They fight one another to see who is the strongest.

Side by side, they spread their front legs for balance and use their necks to push and shove. The first one slams his head into the chest of the other. Now they take turns using their heads like baseball bats! They swing their necks with full force at each other. They could knock each other down, but they rarely do.

After about 15 minutes, one of the two leaves, and everything goes back to normal. The two males rejoin the rest of the herd and eat next to each other peacefully.

Always moving

Giraffes walk in an unusual way. They amble along, moving the two legs on the left side then the two legs on the right side. When they gallop, each stride is about thirteen feet long!

Who leads the group? It is difficult to say. One day, it is one giraffe, another day it is a different one. An adult giraffe likes to be alone some of the time, but it always returns to a group.

During a giraffe's life of 20 to 25 years, it will crisscross the land . . . Africa's living tower.

Even though the neck of the giraffe is long, it has only seven neck bones, called vertebrae. This is the same number as a mouse or a person! The only difference is that each giraffe neck bone is 12 inches long!

Long live the giraffe!

The giraffe is protected in all African countries. Large numbers of giraffes live in reserves and parks in eastern Africa. Unfortunately, in the west, their territory is becoming smaller and smaller. Giraffes are also killed illegally because people want to sell their tails and skins.

Hunted for its meat

For a very long time, African people have hunted only a small number of giraffes for food. Then, at the beginning of this century, hunting for sport became popular with tourists, and the number of giraffes was greatly reduced. Fortunately, parks and reserves were created to protect African wildlife. The future of the giraffe is now brighter than ever because tourists from around the world want to see them.

The giraffe is destroyed by poachers for the bristles of its tail.

Killed for its tail

The giraffe can live in perfect harmony with people and their farm animals. Giraffes rarely damage vegetation and do not eat the same plants as farm animals. But illegal hunting continues. The giraffe is killed because the bristles of its tail are used to make good-luck bracelets and other things to sell.

These vultures will leave only the bones. The people of West Africa use any bones they find to make musical instruments.

Its territory becomes smaller

Little by little, the places for giraffes to live get smaller as people expand their farms and cut down trees for firewood. Giraffes have disappeared from certain regions, and in western Africa they are becoming increasingly rare. In Nigeria and other countries there are special efforts to safeguard them.

A poacher tried to trap this giraffe, but the giraffe broke the rope around its neck and escaped.

Scientific interest

Scientists are interested in studying giraffes and their travels. Some giraffes have been fitted with radio transmitters so that their movements can be recorded.

Other scientists are trying to recognize individual giraffes by their markings. This requires that they make a map of each giraffe's spot patterns . . . not as easy as it sounds!

The giraffe family

Giraffes are mammals that belong to a group called ruminants. Ruminants, such as cows and sheep, chew their cud. A ruminant's stomach has four parts, and its food must be chewed four times!

▲
The *southern giraffe* has markings that are close to the reticulated giraffe of the north.

Giraffes and okapis are the sole survivors of what was once a very large family. Their distant ancestor was the rather short-necked antelope. Over the ages, the neck has become elongated, allowing the giraffe to eat leaves that other animals cannot reach.

Scientists distinguish eight sub-species, each with a difference in the type and color of its coat.

The *masai giraffe* has dark spots in irregular patterns. It lives in Kenya and Tanzania. ▶

▲

The *reticulated giraffe* has large, smooth-sided spots, separated by narrow, white lines. It lives in northeastern parts of Africa.

◀ The *okapi* has the look of a small, brown giraffe with striped legs. Its neck is much shorter than that of its great cousins. Timid and suspicious, it lives alone in the forest. Only a few thousand okapis have been found and counted.

For Further Reading . . .

Giraffe. Caroline Arnold. Photographs by Richard Hewett. William Morrow, 1987.

Giraffe (See How They Grow). Mary Ling. Photographs by Peter Anderson. Dorling Kindersley, 1993.

Giraffes (True Books). Emilie U. Lepthien and Rudolf Steiner. Children's Press, 1996.

Tall Blondes: A Book About Giraffes. Lynn Sherr. Andrews & McMeel, 1997. For older readers.

Use the Internet to Find Out More . . .

The Best Place for Giraffe Links

http://www.trader.com/users/5011/0790/giraf05.htm

This URL was confirmed at the time of publication but may change; we welcome corrections or suggestions for future editions.